VERYAN

how times have changed

FRANK SYMONS

2005

Acknowledgement

The author would like to express his thanks to the publishers, Terry and Neil of Kresenn Kernow, The Cornwall Centre, Alma Place, Redruth.

Cover Photograph: Ken Young of St Agnes

Veryan – How Times Have Changed

© **Frank Symons**

First edition published 2005

Published by:
Palores Publishing
Redruth, Kernow

Designed & Printed by:
St Ives Printing & Publishing Company
High Street, St Ives, Cornwall TR26 1RS, U.K.

ISBN   0-9547985-7-0

CONTENTS

The authors parents

INTRODUCTION

In my other books, I've talked about my life and times here in Veryan, mostly about the past. In this my latest effort, I will endeavour to compare the time when I was growing up with how we live today.

How times have changed

CHAPTER ONE
OUR HOMES and WHAT'S in THEM

I was born and brought up in an old house built of cob. The outer walls were about two feet thick and windows didn't fit properly. This meant it was very draughty and wind, from a certain direction, made the curtains move. The rooms were partitioned with wood and it had a thatched roof.

Five acres of land went with the house and there was a lovely big yard in which the toilet was situated. There was no running water, just a well outside. Heat came from an open fire, Cornish range, for cooking, and a copper in which our clothes were boiled prior to being washed. This copper was in what we called the 'back kitchen.' We also had baths there on a Saturday night.

This room had a concrete floor, as they all did. Other furniture in it included a large table, mangle, for getting excess water out of washed clothes, and a kind of wooden seat, known as a settle. Besides sitting on it there was a high back which could be pulled down to make an extra table. The floor was always scrubbed after washing. From that room one came up two steps and round a wooden screen to the kitchen where a welsh dresser ran the length of one wall. There was also a desk, table, sofa and chairs. Beside the stove there was a black door behind which an old clome oven could be found.

A long pantry was entered through a brown door at the rear of the kitchen. It had a long, thick shelf running down the right hand side and half a barrel stood at the far end for when a pig was killed. The front room had lino on the floor, a table, chairs, sofa and sideboard on which stood the clock my parents received, as a wedding gift, from the Chapel.

Old iron bedsteads stood in the three bedrooms along with wooden wash stands each with a large china basin for washing. There were wardrobes, and the floors were covered with lino. On reflection my parents bed was partly made of wood.

Let's compare that with my flat today. Wall to wall carpets cover the floor and are cleaned with an electric vacuum cleaner. Other electrical aids include, a kettle, iron, razor, radio, cooker, washing machine, television, emersion heater, tape recorder, magnifier and computer. Electric storage heaters keep the place warm and I have a bathroom, with running water and a flush toilet.

It's a far cry from the house in which I grew up. No water to pump, coal to fetch or kindlers to chop, it's always warm and easy to keep clean. When I put my clothes in the machine memories of Mum taking a full day to hand wash often come into my mind. There's no scrubbing floors either, or worrying, 'is the stove going to stay at the correct temperature?'

My radio keeps an even level of sound which was more than could be said of our first wireless. With all these aids, am I any happier than my parents were? I rather doubt it. For most people were very happy and not having had all the things we have now, they didn't miss them.

A cloam oven

CHAPTER TWO
OCCUPANTS of the HOUSES

Most of the cottages were owned by private landlords who let them out at eighteen pence, or two shillings, a week. There were only three or four owner occupiers. A few of the inhabitants were old and most of the tenants had jobs in farming. Two council houses were built in 1944. They had bathrooms, which only three other houses already had. Just after I left school, the first holiday homes arrived, I believe the early fifties brought three of these. There was no pavement then which enabled one old chap to sit in his gateway with his feet in the road. The man living next door to him was a spiritualist who talked about seeing the chamber pots moving.

Four doors away lived a brother and sister who went to work on the same bicycle. They went to Calendra Farm which was reached by going down a steep hill outside our house and up the other side. When having breakfast I would hear them coming, the brother singing *For Ever And Ever*, (a popular song of those days). On reaching our place his sister would mount the bike and hold it steady while brother got on the rear carrier, then off they would go at top speed. Looking back, I'm amazed they never had a serious accident.

A new couple came to live. The man did odd jobs, which included putting in a pane of glass for Mum. He made three trips to a joiner in the next village before getting it cut the correct size. Of an evening men would gather at the allotment or near the end of the village. One old chap, sitting down so long, couldn't get up when leaving. He sat on the bank outside where 'The Bungalow' is now. The villagers were good souls who helped each other in a crisis, more on the subject later.

How different the village is now. There are twenty extra dwellings which makes over sixty, a third of them are empty in winter though. In the old days my parents knew the background of most tenants. These days its more difficult as so few are local.

At Veryan Green, it used to be eighty out of a hundred. That's now down to twenty. As an example, we will look at the council estate in Veryan itself.

When another six were added to two already there in 1948, there was just one person who wasn't Cornish. This was much the same when more were built during the early fifties. In ten houses there were about two non Cornish. Looking at those same dwellings now, its fifty-fifty, locals and incomers. Of the eighteen houses and bungalows built later, the proportion of locals is less, just thirty per cent. In the three private estates, plus the starter homes, locals would only be a quarter of the residents.

Miss Johns outside her home

Bearing in mind in the forties it was eighty out of each hundred, it's not hard to see how the proportion of Cornish has dwindled.

It's the increase in second homes that bothers me most. I can see if this trend isn't stopped, we shall, in twenty years have villages in Cornwall which are only lived in during summer. It's worrying, as the affect on business and schools would be devastating. We already have some in this area with a small number of pupils. Every school closed is one too many and the same applies to shops. Too many have had to shut down in Veryan. For example in the sixties, there were five shops selling food, a filling station and gift shop. All that remains is the gift shop, charity shop, and general store come Post Office. More closures, of any kind, would damage the fabric of village life as I, and many other Cornish folk, have known it. I hope second home owners who read this will understand. I'm not against them personally, just concerned for the future of the rural areas in the county I love.

I make the people who come to reside in Veryan very welcome as many organisations rely on their help to keep going. Since starter homes were built a lot of young families have arrived. This has made the number of pupils at the school, of which I am so proud, higher, which has to be good. Some of the children may choose to remain here and have families of their own.

CHAPTER THREE
WARTIME AND EVACUEES

The bulk of this chapter was written, and sent to me by, Mrs Sayell (Miss Walker). Its an account of the journey which brought the first evacuees to Veryan, in June 1940.

September 1939, found our country once again at war with Germany. I cannot recall much of the early months but can recall my father joining the newly named Home Guard, along with the fact, like everyone who had land, we had to plant potatoes. My parents always got up early, as did the group in this account by my friend Mrs Sayell.

As I recall that morning, a group of adults and children, about sixty in number, was told to gather outside Hornsey Station at 6 am ready for a journey to somewhere.

The children's ages ranged from 4 - 14 and a few school staff were also present. Only two of these would travel. Miss Colbourne, a senior girls teacher, who was in overall charge and Miss Walker, who had recently qualified and joined the staff at South Harringey. That school was to be a Casualty Clearing Station and Miss Walker's classroom, the Mortuary, so it was deemed advisable to move elsewhere.

No one knew our destination, but with no tears or demonstrations of emotion, the mothers said goodbye bravely to their children and we moved off. When we found out the train was taking us to Paddington there was speculation that we were going westward, but again no firm news. A long, long train was waiting at Paddington for us and we were soon away. Gas masks, little cases and serious faces. No mobile phones, magazines or soft drinks, just a few sandwiches each.

Our first stop was Exeter and I recall we were very short of water on the train, so I begged some from the W.R.V.S. ladies. This the children in my carriage shared and the last few drops I sprinkled on my hanky and tried to wipe any smears off the children's faces. People in the country thought that all London children lived in slums and were dirty. I was anxious to make a

11

*Some of the first evacuees to arrive in Veryan, with two of
their teachers, Miss Colbourne and Miss Walker*

good impression when we arrived at wherever we were being sent. A little
while after leaving Exeter, there was great excitement, as the train ran along
beside the sea. One of my six year olds, Owen Tebb, a thoughtful little boy,
said to me, 'Miss Walker, are we still in England?' I was able to reassure him
this was a place called Dawlish, in Devon, and maybe we were nearing the
end of our journey.

The children were tired as it was now nearly 4 pm, but still the train kept
going and it was not until 6 pm that it drew up at Truro station. I think none
of our group had been here before, holidays and weekend breaks were too
expensive. We were told to get into lines and walk up the hill to the girls
school. There each child was given a drink of milk and biscuits, while lined
up outside were a variety of single decker buses. We were told to get in, and
uncomplaining, all the little ones settled down for a further adventure. The
old bus started up and we travelled on, and on, and on. I asked the driver
where we were going and he said, 'You'm some lucky, you'm going to
Veryan, where the sea is nearby'. When I told the children they did cheer up
a little but they were so tired, there was no cheering or shouting.

At about 8 pm, being June it was still light (thank goodness), we pulled up
outside the Legion Hall in Veryan and were asked to go in where we would

be told where we were to be billeted. Here were two wonderful people. Mrs R C Hearle and Miss Jenkin, who were the unendingly kind and efficient billeting officers. They sat at a long table and called out the children's names. Some of the people, on whom the children were to be billeted, lived within walking distance and had come to collect their charges. Otherwise, as petrol was rationed, people had volunteered their cars for taking children, maybe as far as four miles, out to their new homes.

Our children kept disappearing. The girls rapidly, but the boys! I was left, at midnight, with two six year olds. One of the Denyer family and another boy, I think called Arthur Mucklow. Two hollow eyed, scruffy looking, tired little boys. It seemed there was no room anywhere for them, when up spoke a farmer's wife, Mrs Mitchell Osborne. She would take both of them and they would live out on what is now advertised as one of the loveliest views in Britain, at Gwendra Farm.

Having seen the last of my dears settled, I was approached, as I had been several times that evening, by a man (who's accent I couldn't keep up with) who said, if I would come with him in his car, he would take me to my billet.

It was pitch black and I was very tired, so off we went to Churchtown Farm, where Jim and Kit Richards were waiting for me.

The next morning we all went to our first day at Veryan School where Mr Bennett fitted us all in with a minimum of fuss. He was quite a character and never made us feel we were a nuisance. The Cornish people were very kind and the children weren't abused in any way. The Cornish accent, which most of them spoke, took me ages to understand.

Some of the children were rather young to write home, so I wrote their parents once a fortnight, to let them know what was going on. I had been evacuated once before, but never had such a warm welcome as we were given in Veryan and Portloe. I should like to thank those still alive, for the tolerance, patience and kindness. I still love Veryan and often return. Sadly though, one hears very few Cornish accents now.

*Cast iron with cog work
wooden rollers
– the mangle*

*A modern washing
machine/spindryer*

CHAPTER FOUR
THE WOMEN'S ROLE

When I was a boy, most women worked very hard, those with large families especially so. At fourteen, girls left school and did housework. At eighteen, they either joined one of the armed services or the land army. A few went away into factories to make things for the war effort.

Many wives, with husbands away, had sole responsibility for bringing up children. The man, when home again, was head of the house and the bread winner. The wives, with big families, were wonderful. Making do on very low wages, they could all knit and sew, making clothes for children out of adults and passing them from one child to another. They also knew how to salt down a pig, make jam and slow wine or dig vegetables from the garden. I recall seeing many of them struggling up through the village, with a bucket of water in each hand, carrying a skuttle full of coal or faggot of wood. Her life was nothing but work and more work, with spare time almost unknown.

I recall writing in my last book, how, by the time war ended women's lives were beginning to change slightly. Throughout the past six decades they have changed so much that we now have a more independent, liberated fair sex. Some would say they are too liberated, but if I know what's good for me, perhaps I shouldn't agree. They certainly appear less feminine, rarely seen in a skirt or dress, as was the norm years ago. Whether all this being liberated has made them easier, or more difficult, to get along with I simply can't say, as not being married, I don't have to live with one.

Let's look at the advantages they have over the ladies of my young days.

Most have a job, a car and bank account. Husbands help with the children, the household chores and the shopping. Window cleaners are employed, some husbands do the decorating, a few even get their own meals, good gracious me, and one or two fetch the children from school. If a woman chooses to leave her husband, not only can she claim maintenance but half of what they own is also hers. No wife, having left her husband, should be left with nothing, but I feel a bit more moderation might be a good thing.

Modern rayburns or older rayburns and agas converted to gas (above) and electric cookers have replaced the traditional Cornish ranges like the one below

I've no problem with women in top jobs and certainly don't oppose women priests, and when all is said and done why shouldn't ladies be equal. They've already, in the course of writing this chapter, been upgraded, from women to ladies. Most of the time, I like them, when they try to boss me though, I feel glad to be single. When all is said and done, what would we men do without them?

CHAPTER FIVE
OUTINGS

During the war outings were rare, an afternoon on the beach maybe, or a trip to town for an eye test, the latter quite frequent. The odd concert at the Church or Chapel and that was about it.

I can recall on one occasion, a Whitsun Monday to be precise, Dad was coming home from work at midday and we were all off to the beach. We never got there though, for as he came up round the corner a thunder storm broke and it poured with rain.

The beach

After the war we started going to the Camborne Horse Show each August Bank Holiday. 1946 saw Beryl, the elder of our two evacuee girls, down on holiday. My Uncle also wanted to go, so, Dad hired Mr Morse's big car in which two extra could sit in the back on foldaway chairs, and off we went. Beryl, who would have been eighteen at the time, was wearing a maroon dress, with a white plastic belt, which she had made herself.

It was during that stay that I took a cigarette from her bag, tried to smoke it and made myself sick. That's enough secrets for the moment.

The Legion Hall

I also recall going to Probus Feast once where there were sports including cycle racing. At the horse show we watched two riders who I recall clearly. They were Mr Walter Rail, of Budock, with three horses: Early Morn, Nosey Parker and Johnny Walker. The other was Mr J T Roberts. His horses names were: Spider, Mac and Brian. It was Mr Roberts' son, Tredge, who rode them I think.

At Camborne, there was always a parade of all the cattle, described by Mr W T H Christophers, then secretary of Cornwall N.F.U. He would say something about each breed as it passed the grandstand.

During the fifties we went once a year to some of Dad's cousins at Treverva. They lived next door to Mr Edgar Kessell who conducted the Treverva Male Voice Choir, among others.

School didn't go on trips until after I had left, which was just as well, for some big families had three or four children going at the same time, and might not have been able to pay for such a luxury.

What a difference these days with trips much further afield, which cost real money. Some children from bigger than average families still get left out, which would be good enough for me, not liking such escapades.

At the age of eleven I had my first bicycle. Now I could go and see my Uncles and Aunts, trips of two or three miles. I also went to Truro on my own from the age of about ten.

Life was much more simple then, and we didn't expect to be on the go, as children do now. I find it sad though they can't go far alone, as we were able to. They have outings galore, but always accompanied by an adult. Going places is now normal and not just once a month, its nearly every day. The car has of course made such a thing possible, plus the fact adults don't work nearly so many hours.

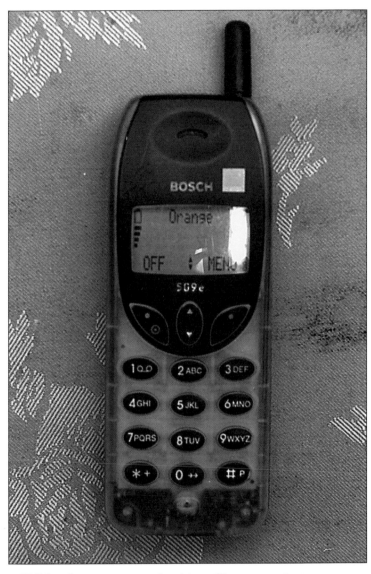

Children's presents can be things like, computers, cameras, video players, bicycles or the more expensive, mobile phones, which cost money to run

CHAPTER SIX
CHRISTMAS PARTIES

What we didn't get from outings was made up for at Christmas. Dad was the eldest of seven so there were lots of relatives to visit. At one house we played *Pontoon* for matches, in a small front room, with a Tilly lamp. Nuts were cracked by placing one on the floor and jumping on it, and if one was took short, the loo was outside in the dark.

I can recall stumbling across dark fields, quite late at night. At Trewartha Chapel the prizes were always given out at the years end when we had tea and a party. We often played a game called *Poor Pussy.*

In it a nominated person had to kneel in front of one of the others and meow like a cat. If they made the person laugh, they took over. Some of the noises were awful, and nothing like a cat, but they brought howls of laughter from everyone.

Another game was *Postman's Knock,* during which us boys would endeavour to get some unsuspecting girl out into the porch, so we could kiss her. Someone stood by the door, and as each girl had a number, we had to pick the right one. If a girl didn't want to be kissed, things could get awkward.

Duster Hockey was a rough old game in which two teams opposed one another. One member from each would have a stick, with which he would try to get the duster up the other end while the other did all he could to stop him. It could, and often did, get very rough, with sticks flying all over the place. But this was nothing to the noise generated by about a hundred children who attended the British Legion party each year.

The Legion hall would be packed and the din was enough to burst one's eardrums. I believe we were given an orange and small bar of chocolate. The W I party was rather more sedate, with plenty of members to keep us in order. Each took provisions for the children they had invited, they were pooled, and we all had a good tea. I can still see the enormous kettles now, put to boil on the two open fires, set in the wall backing on to the farmyard. The whole thing took place under the oil lamps hanging from the ceiling and there wasn't always enough light to see what was going on. At one such party I was persuaded to sing. My choice was *The First Noelle* I did so in a room so gloomy, we might have all been out in the fields with the shepherds.

Some 52 years later I went to a party for the older folk, in other words we were all past the first flush of youth. Put on by members of the committee, who run what is now known as the parish hall, it was held in a well lit room, far removed from anything of my childhood. With electricity, a kitchen, cloakrooms and gas heating, I marvelled at the changes as I recalled those parties of long ago. There was never any alcohol, very different from these days, and Christmas didn't cost much either.

Let's take a look at some costs. We had our own poultry, and most of the vegetables, those not grown by Dad, were brought from the farm where he worked. So, only the pudding ingredients had to be paid for, and the coal for the stove, of course. A holly bush was our Christmas tree and decorations were kept from year to year. One didn't have many sweets as they were rationed and no fruit could be bought from overseas. Dad sometimes brought a few medlars, from my grandparents farm. Christmas was much more of a religious festival, when most of us, remembered the birth of Jesus.

I do recall the first time we heard King George through our new wireless. Since then, the real meaning of Christmas has been gradually pushed into the background, by too much commercialisation, and drinking. There can't be a party now without someone getting drunk.

It's also a time when people feel the urge to get into debt with a plastic card. Children's presents can be things like, computers, cameras, video players, bicycles or the more expensive, mobile phones, which cost money to run. One such present will cost more than a dozen families had in my childhood. It's all gone to the extreme and I would much rather have Christmas as I knew it when a boy.

CHAPTER SEVEN
OUR WORKING LIVES

In the early days of my life, most of the men in Veryan worked on the farms of which there were forty or so in the parish. They still worked six days a week though that soon became five and a half. Agriculture in this parish would have meant a living for some one hundred families, as farming was very labour intensive then.

The first tractors had arrived pre-war with the Fordson. The Ferguson followed in the forties and by the early fifties, balers and combine harvesters had come too. Many farmers had a milking machine and cow herds began to grow.

People were now going further to find employment. Men went by lorry to the china clay pits, in the St Austell area, while on the roads they still worked in their own area, where each man had so much to keep trimmed and the ditches clean.

Several boats still went to sea from Portloe, catching fish for a living. There were usually two men in each boat. Everyone but the very old had a job of some kind, often walking some distance to do a half days work. As stated under *The Women's Role* most young people left school at 14 during the war, and 15 soon after. With large families parents were glad to have the extra money coming in. Girls doing domestic work would have earned about ten shillings a week, boys on a farm a bit more.

My generation saw the latter taking up apprenticeships, a good many with a firm of builders at Portscatho. One boy even rode a bicycle to St Mawes where he learnt plumbing. Though young they had to go on a bicycle in all winds and weathers. The thrifty ones put money aside and bought a motor cycle when old enough to ride one. It took five years to learn a trade in those days, but most of them learnt well and many went on to run a business of their own. Many of the young people who were a few years my senior had to help with the war effort. Young men who weren't engaged in agriculture joined one of the services. One or two even went as Bevan boys down the coal mines. The young ladies alternative to the forces was the land army.

Farm workers enjoy their crowst

Sixty years on, working hours are shorter, and work much easier. Machines have taken over and even on the farms most of the very hard work has gone. In the old days it took a man with a team of horses a full day to plough an acre of land. It can be done now, on a tractor, in a few minutes with no effort. The corn harvest, which used to go on for ever, or so it seemed, is done in no time now.

Young people go on to higher education and most of them don't work until well over twenty. Veryan is home to a different type of worker, nurses, teachers, and even a dental surgeon. They all commute miles every day which is so easy now almost everyone has a car. There was a time when two of our parishioners commuted to London and returned at weekends. The days when Truro was thought a long way off are very much a thing of the past. If one is not one hundred per cent fit, money can be obtained without doing a stroke.

There is also 'Social Security,' which in a low wage county like Cornwall, can leave one better off not doing anything. When in the village shop I see many working age men there. That wouldn't have been possible in the forties. Two Nursing Homes, within a four mile radius, make jobs for between seventy and eighty. That wasn't the case when I was a boy either. One type of job has gone and another new one taken its place.

Many of life's changes are not to my liking. The fact people have easier working lives though, most certainly is. As a boy I saw middle aged people bent double with hard work. I saw others working when not fit to be out of bed. Failure to do so would have meant no money coming into their house. They worked in all weathers with just a couple of hessian sacks to keep them dry. No wonder so many died young. That was sixty years ago, but memories of such things prompt me to say, 'Thank god, it doesn't happen today.'

In order to give a balanced view though, is too much money now handed out to those who do nothing? Or have things gone too far the other way?

*A double furrow plough, one of many such pieces of
agricultural history that have now been replaced by
mechanized equipment*

Veryan school above and below a modern Personal Computer, something that every pupil in today's school has access to

CHAPTER EIGHT
CHILDREN'S LIVES

Children under five didn't go out like they do these days for there were no nursery schools. So some who had been reared on outlying farms scarcely knew any other children when they started school. Even at five getting there could mean a long walk, and the day didn't end until 3.45 pm. For those coming, say two miles, it meant a very long day.

Classrooms weren't warm like they are now either and teachers were much more strict. Five year olds got shouted at and even spanked for bad behaviour, while older children got caned by the headmaster, with a short thick cane plus a longer thin one. Such action, these days would, land him in court and even a teacher who shouts at a child is frowned on.

While on the subject of school, unlike now, it was very rare for a child to be suspended or expelled. These days most children attend nursery school before beginning their education at four. Ninety per cent are taken by Mum in the family car. At eleven they continue their education at a comprehensive, after which, most of them go on to sixth form college. Being taken to both by bus.

The softly-softly approach forced on teachers is also common in most homes where discipline has gone out of the window. Parents of the forties, who spanked and caned their children on a regular basis, would think today's far too soft. While I have no children, and deplore any form of cruelty, it seems to me, its now gone from one extreme to the other.

'They must be allowed to express themselves' is what I hear. Any response I could make would, I fear, be very rude, so I say nothing. While as a child, I had to walk everywhere, these days children don't walk the length of their nose. The car is ever present, taking them hither and thither at the drop of a hat. Trips into town, which for us were a real luxury, are now taken for granted, as are swimming lessons, drama, ballet, music, riding horses, you name it, the kids of today do it. On leaving school, a car of their own is a must, with no thought of how they can afford to run it. At that age we would have had a bicycle, on which to reach our first job. A car or even motorcycle, one had to save up for.

Lots of us had little jobs well before we left school. Two friends and I had our own garden at the allotment, at eleven. Three of my friends caught rabbits and sold them, another boy went round with the baker on a Saturday, while one of my best friends worked weekends on a farm. On top of little jobs we all ran errands and chopped kindlers to light the fire. Parents today are much better off and the law prevents children working anyway. But was it such a bad thing? I don't think so.

Computers have become part of every child's life, as has television, videos and every expensive aid with which to keep them amused. But for all their wealth of material things, there is one thing missing today, which my generation took so much for granted. Yes, you have guessed it. The freedom to roam. To wander for miles with not an adult in sight.

A changed society has meant the freedom we enjoyed is no longer possible. A parent, or parents, accompany children wherever they go, even two or three hundred yards to school. I can recall during a holiday in Northampton, when ten years old, walking on my own, to a playground some way from my Uncle's home, and staying there for hours. That was in a big town and nobody worried about my safety. So maybe I am being unfair to the children of today, who have so much and yet no freedom.

Here in Veryan most of the children are very good and I am blessed to have three great youngsters next door.

In conclusion, I get asked 'would I change my young life, for that of a child today?' My reply: 'certainly not,' for no amount of costly toys etc, could make up for the freedom that was so much part of my life.

In a way, not having too much, prepared us well for the real world, where one can't always have everything. The fact most children now have far too much, makes me wonder how will they cope if hard times come?

To sum up, I don't think there's really much wrong with children or young people today. Of course they have faults but no doubt older folk in the forties thought the same of my generation.

To be honest, I know full well we certainly weren't perfect.

CHAPTER NINE
MUSIC

From an early age I was taken to Chapel and quickly came to know, and love, a great many Hymns. We sang one at Sunday School called, *Have you had a kindness shown, pass it on*, and I recall singing, *The Lords My Shepherd* as a solo, at the Sunday School Aniversary.

My Mum played the organ at Trewartha Chapel for well over seventy years, from the age of eight. Her brother Tom, sang in the Northampton Choral Society for some time, and with his wife, in their chapel choir.

Male voice choirs came and gave concerts at the chapel. I recall Treverva, among others, along with the Camborne Centenary Quartet. We always listened to *Sunday Half Hour*, on the wireless, if the battery would still provide the power. This was preceded by *Grand Hotel*, with Albert Sandler, and the orchestra.

I always felt proud when the National Anthem was played, and still love the patriotic songs written during the war. I recall *There'll Always Be An England,* along with so many more which I have on tapes. I play them often, in memory of the brave souls who gave the ultimate sacrifice, their lives.

Music turns me on. Especially a Welsh rugby crowd singing, *Land Of My Fathers,* or *Trelawney,* sung by a Cornish choir. Either can, and do, move me to tears. I also love the music from the musicals, sung in my young days by Ann Ziggler, Webster Booth, the great Paul Robeson, Walter Midgley and Gracie Fields, to name but a few.

There was an American programme, *Big Bill Cambell's, Rocky Mountain Rhythm*, which Dad and I listened to on Sunday afternoons. The type of thing now called Country & Western. Bill Cambell would sometimes say a monologue. One I recall was, *The Old Cane Bottom Chair.*

Popular songs after the war included, *Now Is The Hour, You Are My Sunshine* and from musicals, *This Is My Lovely Day, Some Enchanted Evening* and *We'll Gather Lilacs.*

Popular music these days is a closed book to me, but one mustn't criticise. Every generation is different and the young people of today, most likely, don't think much of the music I love so much.

As I believe in, live and let live, I shan't enlarge on the subject.

The pupils learn music at Veryan School

CHAPTER TEN
FOOD

From the age of three what I ate was governed by what was, and wasn't, rationed. We were all given a ration book with coupons for each item that came in for this rationing. The quota per week, for each person wasn't much, and one had to register with the grocer you intended purchasing from.

We were registered with Miss Rundle who lived here in Veryan Green. Most houses had a garden, mainly in the local allotments, where lots of vegetables were produced. Potatoes were planted in a farmers field, and a few hens kept, where a family had room. Some people fattened a pig, but as I've told of its killing before, we won't labour the point.

Having our own milk, eggs, cream and the odd hen, which could be killed, we didn't go short. In fact, when our evacuee girl's mother came down to see them, she had a shock to find they had put on weight. Dad got a shock too, when he found fault with the bread and butter she was cutting. He arrived home from work, took a look at her, and exclaimed: 'What do you call that?' 'Bread and butter, of course,' came her reply. 'More like bread and scrape,' said Dad. She turned on him and said, bluntly: 'You live like fighting cocks. We only have 2 ounces of butter a week.' Father looked like a man shot at and no more was said.

Children were expected to eat what was put in front of them or go without, including rabbit pie and a fair amount of potatoes. When school meals started if any of us said we didn't like something, the teacher would say: 'There are thousands of people who would be glad to have it.' Potatoes weren't rationed, but meat was. That's where our poultry came in handy. Their eggs were useful for breakfast and cooking. New items appeared in Miss Rundle's shop, such as dried egg and black treacle, while the butcher told the girls and I, 'Tell your mother, it's a piece of a dog, this week.' I believe some of us walked to Portloe, now and again, to buy fish.

My Gran, who lived with us, often had what she called: 'Kidley Broth' for supper. Hot water, with bread, salt, and pepper. We also liked bread and milk. Dad had bacon with fried potatoes for breakfast, while we children often had porridge. There were very few sweets on ration and fresh fruit only in season. I wonder where Mum got the bacon which Dad ate, possibly most of the six rations. He was often walking after the horses all day and needed good food.

Nobody studied the calories in those days and the medical people weren't so obsessed with keeping people slim. There wasn't much chance of getting an expanded girth, like mine, as most folk worked hard and had lots of exercise.

Cooking wasn't easy with the Cornish range. The heat couldn't be controlled and if the wind suddenly got up, a cake could get burnt, or go down in the middle.

Few had enough money to even think about going out for a meal. There was nowhere much to get one anyway, until after the war.

I often wonder, when looking back, how the young people of today would cope with rationing. Especially when I hear mothers asking their children what they want for tea?

Many are right fussy what they eat. A product of society today, where there's too much of everything and youngsters get what they want. Cooking is easier as appliances can be regulated. There's no kindlers to be chopped, or coal to be fetched. With a microwave, meals can be ready in a matter of minutes, and ready cooked ones taken from the freezer.

Most wives now have a job and don't have the time to prepare a meal as my Mum did. Children live on convenience food, such as burgers, and chips, with many schools giving a choice. When one buys a joint of beef, there's hardly any fat on it, and no knowing what the animal has eaten, or what was put on the land where it was grown.

When I first lived alone, ready cooked meals were sometimes bought from a van which came once a week. One day, I picked up what I thought was roast chicken. But, when I tried to eat it, the top of my mouth was almost removed by its contents. Like many products these days, it had been spiced up, which didn't impress me, so I've kept well away from such things. I like good old Cornish cooking, which lies in you, not this modern stuff.

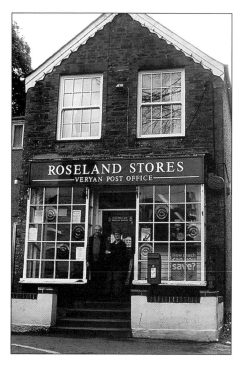

*The Roseland Stores
& Post Office*

Much of our food these days is tinkered with, to keep us free from germs, but we have lost any immunity we ever had through being over cautious.

Vegetables have to be washed before they are sold and most food is wrapped and double wrapped. We drank milk straight from the cow and men working in the fields, took a pasty from their bag, and ate it, without any thought of washing their hands. I fear it's hygiene gone mad. With so many laws concerning the sale of food it must drive retailers insane.

There are so many places where a meal can be bought and most people go out for a meal on a regular basis. When told, by a lady how she paid £22 for a meal, my reply was: 'I could live for a week on that.'

In my heart I am so glad to see people better off, but it's a far cry from the forties, when many scarcely had enough money to keep body and soul together. Who says, we aren't better off? We are, whatever people say.

One shouldn't forget either, that going out to meals, makes employment.

From the 1930's Roadster (left) to the AC Cobra's (below) and through to today's large engined cars the improvements in transport have allowed for greater accessibility to the villages of the Roseland

CHAPTER ELEVEN
TRANSPORT

The main form of transport during my childhood, was the bicycle, and most households had at least one. Most men used one for going to and from work and some children rode one to school. We did have a good bus service, which went to Truro three days a week and St Austell two.

The drivers would purchase goods for anyone who was unable to go for some reason. The buses were both owned by local people, who knew many of their passengers, and though old bone shakers, always arrived at their destination. One of the owners told me, many years later, he often stayed up all night in order to have his fit for the road next day. For, if he didn't go, he would have no money to live on. The buses were always full, with people standing, but the drivers always managed to squeeze one more in. Thinking back, it amazes me they were so full. There were four or five trips to Truro, on each of the three days, but of course, it was the only way of getting there.

By the end of that decade, there were more cars than when it had started, here in Veryan. There could have been a dozen by 1950, which is nothing compared to the present day.

I shall be accused of sour grapes, because, due to my sight, I can't have one, but its reached the point now, where the numbers are not a joke. Everywhere one looks, especially in the evenings, there's a car parked on every bit of spare ground, by the roadside, and even on private property. During summer, it's nothing new for me to come back from a walk, or get up of a morning, to find a car parked on my forecourt. As this was put there, at some expense, for cars coming to my shop, I don't find it funny.

I'm not against anyone parking for a few minutes, or in an emergency, but all night is another matter. The parking problem is the same in most towns and villages and needs sorting out. Putting up the prices of fuel, hurts the poorer people, and I don't agree with it. Nor do I think road tax very fair.

If I were clever enough to know the answer I'd probably be a very rich man. The idea of getting people back on public transport is talked about, but one has to consider the vast difference, between urban, and rural areas. In the latter, where people travel miles each day, to find employment it simply doesn't work.

Transport is something, which has really changed in sixty years, and the car has become a must for most families. To help the few, who don't, or can't, have one, there are various services available, driven mainly by volunteers, they pick people up, and take them anywhere, at quite a low cost. I have used one myself, and was very pleased with it. A Taxi, which in the forties, would take one to Truro, for about £1, would now cost that, or more, for one mile.

An old British motorcycle

CHAPTER TWELVE
A KIND and CARING VILLAGE

I was born into a Christian family, where kindness and consideration for others was the order of the day. Mum was always helping someone, and I recall how one day she removed a bead from the nose of a little girl who lived a hundred yards away. My parents were good to the evacuee girls, who I still hear from 64 years on. I recall many a kindness, shown to us, when I was a boy.

The friend, who helped Dad with the potatoes, also helped me a lot when I first had a piece of Dad's allotment, giving much good advice. There was the kind family, who fed Dad and I, when Mother was in hospital, along with the dear old soul, who came to stay, while taking care of us for two weeks. Miss Rundle, who kept the grocers shop, was more than kind when I first set up in business. Letting me have her garden, use the shop scales, and even her telephone. The farmer who gave me casual work on his farm, which really helped until I earned a full living.

At Sunday School, we came upon and loved *Have You Had A Kindness Shown, Pass It On.* Wonderful words, which I've never forgotten. We were often told to 'Do as you would be done by.' This stuck in my mind, and I've tried, in my dealings with the public, so to do. A strong faith has also influenced my life and it still does today.

In those far off days, when I was growing up, money was scarce and we had to make do. Wartime of course, bound us together, as only adversity can. Having to go without was no bad thing. The folk who were so good with help, will always have a place in my memory, and be held in high esteem.

Are people so kind, and caring today? In my experience: yes, I think they have been throughout my life. The kind man, who came, so willingly, during my mental illness, and the dear lady, who took me to the hospital, when I was having E.C.T.'s, were from the sixties and 70, feeling low at the time, they have a special place in my heart. All those, who gave kind words, when I took over running the shop from Mum. There are so many I could mention.

37

A modern Nursing Home

Fifteen years ago, my parents were both seriously ill at the same time, and peoples' kindness quite overwhelmed me. Five of them stayed up a night, so I could rest. Three helped in the shop, a good many brought food, and at least 20 offered transport when Mum went into hospital, where she died. Though under great strain, I felt they all cared.

1992 saw Father in a Nursing Home, which brought more kind friends. Two of my classmates, at school, took me to see him at least twenty times each. When six months later, he passed away, another came from Exeter to help carry him. So, I can say, quite honestly Veryan remains a very caring community.

As I write now in the 21st century that kindness is still about. The ladies, who help in my shop, the lovely gentleman, who drove me to computer class, along with its tutor, and assistant. Those who take me to the doctor, the friend, who for thirty years, has always been there for me, need I go on. When quiet, I often sit, and just count the many blessings life has brought me.

On a much wider theme, I feel we should all count our blessings more often. My charity shop was set up in gratitude for all life has given me. I meet some wonderful people and have made a lot of friends. Knowing they care makes life so worthwhile in a world so full of hatred, where money rules.

If I could have one wish before I pass on, it would be to replace the hatred, with love and kindness.

CHAPTER THIRTEEN
HOSPITALS

I had my first stay in hospital late in 1938, when at the age of two, I had a hernia operation. As I can't recall a thing about that one, it's best we move on nine years, to the summer of 1947, and a beautiful one it was. I spent most of August at the old City Hospital, or Infirmary, as it was often known. It was the same thing as before and I wasn't very charmed with the place, and all the rules.

Visiting was on Wednesday and Saturday afternoons, and my parents weren't allowed to see me for about twelve days. Some of the nurses were alright, others were a bit bossy, the ward Sister ruled with a rod of iron. Coming round to see each patient every day. Sometimes the Matron came, in her white cap and navy dress.

There was a cleaning lady, called Mrs Hill, who lived at Daniel Road. She wore a blue overall and would read to me for a while, after work. A nurse named Kurnick, often did the same, I really liked her. There was another, well built nurse, who was a bit *John Blunt*, and a small one called Nurse Tuck. There were sets of earphones on each of the the twenty odd beds on which the radio could be heard, but the less said concerning the food, the better.

There was a boy next to me called, Kenneth, who had been bitten by an Adder. He was given injections, which must have hurt a lot, for it took two nurses to hold him. I recall he spent much time hurling pillows at them afterwards. It was the Male Surgical Ward which opened, at the far end on to a balcony, that was home to three or four beds. One of the chaps, a young fellow named Lawrence, had to lie on his back for thirteen weeks. His sister would come to see him of an evening and always spoke to me.

Mother and I, had dinner at the Galleon, in Victoria Square, where she worked many times afterwards. Each morning the beds were pulled out, so the floor could be polished, which made it rather slippery. I went in on the Saturday and waited four days for something to happen. On the Wednesday evening two nurses put screens round me. They rolled me over on my back, and stuck a rubber tube up my bottom. This tube had a round funnel on its end into which soapy water was poured. One ran off and came back with a bedpan, which she shoved under me. Just as well she had, for what I thought was an operation, turned out to be an enema.

Next morning, I was got ready and taken away on a trolley. I awoke back in my bed with padding where they had operated. Next day, when Sister came round, she told me I had to stay in bed for two weeks. A Mr Thomas, was on the other side of me, and when his friend came in, I was moved nearer the balcony end, next to Mr Duffy.

The Sisters name was Wright and the nurses wore green uniforms. One night some of the more mobile men, went out on the balcony. One of them had a radio and there was boxing on. On returning, one of them told me, Freddie Mills had beaten Gus Lesnavitch. It meant nothing to me at the time. Nurse Tuck had taken my stitches out after a few days. Small, with very black hair, I think she was Irish. Mum came twice a week, brought *Dandy*, my comic, and read about *Black Bob* the sheepdog to me.

At last, they allowed me to get up, and I dashed round the ward in a wheelchair the first day. They were pretty strict about visitors, who dare not stay an extra minute, and woe betide anyone who sat on the bed. At last the day to leave came, and I said goodbye to my favourite nurse, along with Mrs Hill. Mum went in twice in 1949, when evening visiting had been introduced. Only half an hour though.

What a difference I found, when in 1994, I broke my wrist, and had to stay in 48 hours. The doctor called himself Nigel and the Sister, Helen. Visitors sat on the beds and came and went as they pleased. The food had improved, if only I had two hands with which to cut the meat, and one got a menu for the next meal. I enjoyed teasing the nurses and chatting with John, opposite, who had lost a leg. The whole atmosphere was much more relaxed and I quite liked it. One thing I didn't enjoy, was having my arm in a sling, pulled up and fixed to a wooden frame above my head. Dressing myself with one hand was a pain, but after a struggle, I did it.

So, on the whole, I thought hospitals were better than during my child-hood.

CHAPTER FOURTEEN
THE TOURIST TRADE

There weren't many tourists during the forties. Most of the ones who did come, arrived at Truro station, and only a few had cars. Many more arrived in the following decade, when there were several campers, and a few people, Mum among them, took in bed and breakfast.

One Sunday, there was a gale, a young couples tent blew down, so they came to us for the night. Mum also had a party from Yorkshire, consisting of two men and three ladies, the latter all slept in one bed.

On another occasion, two married couples wanted to sleep in the same room, and a young couple brought their boat, on a weak looking cart, which broke down the first time they went out. Then we had a party of four who ate a whole chicken when Mum took it in.

During the forties, one could go to the beach and almost have it to yourself. Once more cars arrived in summer, that soon changed. There were two campsites in farmers fields; one run by The Blamey's at Carne, the other by the Richards at Tregenna and of course holiday homes had started. The local buses went on day trips, of which I recall going to Lands End at the age of 12. Few houses had a bathroom, and I recall Mum taking a large jug of hot water upstairs, so the visitors could wash. One chap threw it out of the window when he'd finished.

These days, the tourist trade is big business, with registered Caravan sites and a car park at Carne beach. The Nare Hotel, is much bigger, as most are. They now open most of the year and employ a lot of staff. Kelly's Ice Cream comes to the beach as they have for decades and there are notices on display concerning dogs and powerboats. People arrive in summer, from many parts of the county, which along with lots of tourists makes it very busy.

As Cornwall needs them, more than ever with so many past occupations gone we have to put up with the traffic. Many new attractions have been started which in turn makes the roads where they're situated extremely busy. Truro for example, which is bad enough at any time of year, becomes absolute chaos on a wet day in summer. As a greengrocer, in my working life, the tourists brought a lot of money into my shop and though I get cross when they park on my forecourt without asking these days on the whole I welcome them as their presence helps most business people both in Veryan and throughout the county.

Some have become my friends, and a good many send a card at Christmas. One or two have been coming to my shop, since it began 40 years ago, Mother was running it then, and it pleases me when they remember her.

Our lives are a wheel, within a wheel, and we all live in some way through helping each other. Though, I agree, the tourists aren't all perfect the locals aren't perfect either, life for me, is about getting along with people treat them right and in most cases they will do likewise.

CHAPTER FIFTEEN
MY MEMORIES of WARTIME

In an earlier chapter I gave Mrs Sayell's account of the journey she made from London with a party of evacuees. In this chapter I would like to recall some memories of my own.

They begin on the night two of the group mentioned arrived at our house. Their stay with us has been well documented in an earlier book so I won't dwell on it. Instead I will start by recalling some of the other new arrivals in Veryan parish during the war. Annandale, a large house quite near where I now live, had several, as I found out recently. One of the girls who I do recall rang me one Sunday. Her name was Evelyn and another girl, Irene, was there at the same time. During a two hour conversation I discovered at least half a dozen more children had also been billeted there. I assume before or after them.

Evelyn is now one of seven I keep in touch with. Ann and Jean Walter arrived later and after a short stay in billets there Mum came and took a cottage. The same thing happened with Norman, David and Keith Kent, who ended up living at Portloe.

Others in that village included Margaret, Myra and Pamela. Norman was at Carne Farm with Jean and Donald close by on another farm. Terry Johnson was billeted at Veryan Vicarage and the senior London teacher at Rose Villa, near the Roseland Stores. Another friend of mine, Leslie Pollard, says he had the best billets. He lived happily with the Johns family at Carragaloose Farm and Barbara Elton stayed with another Johns at Camels. There were quite a few on farms quite a way from Veryan village. The ones who spring to mind include Beryl, and Pamela Wills, along with four children by the surname of Howard, who were on farms at Treworlas.

John and Edward Watts, along with Reg Cook, found themselves on another farm at Ruan Highlanes. The Watts boys had a sister, Maureen, who was billeted quite near them. She lived with the Higmans and returns each year for holidays with their daughter Mona, now Mrs Pearce. Jean

Walter married my friend David Pearce and they now live in Exeter. Some of the children helped on the farms on which they were billeted.

Leslie Pollard recalls helping when the threshing machine came, and getting paid for it. He also remembers catching rabbits and many other things. These include being late back from school one day having spent some time with our other evacuee Shirley, one would hardly call it courting, at nine years old. Such things did enter the children's minds though for one nine year old, described Miss Walker as a: 'Lovely bit of stuff.' My cousin called girls 'old maids' and kept away from them.

That's enough abuse for the ladies. I recall the presence of evacuees with great affection, and their teachers with respect. I also recall how hard my Dad worked planting the potatoes, as everyone with land had to do. Already working a six day week it meant a lot of evening work for Dad. Having ploughed the land earlier he would bring my Granddad's horse and cart home with him and borrow implements from a nearby farmer. The land would be worked down and the furrows drawn out with the help of a friend. An implement known as a banker was used for this after which manure was thrown into the furrows with a fire shovel from the cart. The same friend helped Dad cut the potatoes which were large enough. They were then placed in baths for taking to the field very early the next day. Some ladies from the village would drop them before Dad brought the horse home once more and covered them with the banker. When lifting time came the same ladies would help and father did then have a day off. They were put in fifty six pound sacks and picked up by the wholesaler.

War brought much sadness to those who lost loved ones. A boy at school lost his dad while two girls lost their brother. The Chapel caretaker, Mrs Frost, lost her son George and never really got over it. When she grew old I often went to see her and always found a very sad lady, on Remembrance Sunday. 'Don't like this old day boy' she would say. I tried to understand, but how could I for she had given so much. It always made me feel very humble and even now, thirty years on, I still think of her when the day comes round. Throughout those dark days one hymn was sung often at Chapel:-

Holy father in thy mercy
Hear our anxious prayer
Keep our loved ones, now far distant
Neath thy care.

The war brought many servicemen and women to Veryan along with Land Girls. In the darkest hours there was still time for romance. Those days were no exception as the men married local girls and the land army young ladies charmed farmer's sons. Each year when someone comes into my shop and says: 'I was evacuated here, during the war,' the memories come flooding back. They are a link with my childhood, which with the passing years, grow even more precious.

Veryan Church

Section of the Home Guard, Veryan, 1940.
Mr Bennett in charge; Mr Fuge second in command

Portloe and District Band circa 1932. Conductor Joe Chenoweth

CHAPTER SIXTEEN
PLACES OF WORSHIP

I was brought up a Methodist and taken to Trewartha chapel at an early age. Mother played the organ there as she had for many years. It was part of what was known as The Roseland Circuit which consisted of ten chapels. They were as follows St Mawes, St Just, St Antony, Gerrans, Philliegh, Ruan, Port Holland, Portloe, Trewartha and Ebenezer.

Many of them had a Sunday School as did our Chapel when I first went. The outbreak of war saw a room full of children but in ten years the number had fallen to six. I still have in my home a Bible received from Trewartha in 1946, I treasure it, and feel sad today's children don't have a Sunday school to which they can go.

I recall going to concerts at Ruan on many a Good Friday and Harvest Festivals at Ebenezer. They were for us boys, shame on us, a lot of fun. There was always a chairman and a speaker which by the time they both had their say took ages. Afterwards the sale of produce took place. Miss Rundle also ran the village shop which gave her access to food on ration. As already mentioned some of her customers were poor and didn't take up their ration. This meant she could take things which were hard to come by and sell them there. Us boys would bid for things at times with money we didn't have. Someone always bid higher but I often wonder how we would have felt if landed with something to pay for.

Now and then if there was no Sunday School Dad and I would go over there of a Sunday afternoon. This happened one day when Mr Mitchell sat behind us. A hymn was given out and the organ began to play. But it wasn't the tune he liked. So instead of singing he kept saying 'Wrong tune, wrong tune' The shell of the Chapel is still there I pass it often which brings back many memories. All the Chapels I knew as the Roseland Circuit no longer have services which would break Mums heart, were she alive. The Sunday Schools have also left us so the children don't get the chance to learn about Jesus light of the world His name, which has lit up my life, is rarely heard in a world that needs him so much. The faith instilled in me at a young age has brought me through many bad times and my life would be nothing without it.

Veryan Churh was strong in the forties and also had a Sunday School in fact there weren't many children who didn't attend, even if their parents never attended a place of worship.

At School the day always began with a Hymn and a prayer and we said *The Lords Prayer*, before leaving. It was always a Church school but don't recall going over there many times. I recall two Deaconesses coming to the circuit and attending something called Sunshine Corner. It started with the following chorus:

> *Sunshine corner, oh its very fine*
> *Just for children, under ninety nine*
> *All are welcome, every seat is free*
> *Trewartha sunshine corner, is the place for me.*

A couple named Mason came to live at Trewartha, just after the war. Mrs Mason played the piano at Sunday school ,and brought some of the Pearce family with her. It was the start of a fifty eight year friendship with David. A painting of the Chapel hangs on my wall, a gift to my parents, on their Golden Wedding anniversary.

CHAPTER SEVENTEEN
MY CONCLUSIONS

There have, as I've shown, been many changes during my lifetime, some good, others some of which the reader will have guessed by now, I don't like. Let's take a look at those which have made our lives better first. Modern technology allows me to type these words, and save them on my computer, what a boon these are to people with impaired vision.

Washing machines are also a big help. Computers can have their bad side though, where children are allowed free access. Getting about is easier, but there are far too many cars, for comfort. When I visit a friend, in a home, how well it compares, with the poor man I recall, who spent his last days, in an old bus. My friend is happy, and I think that's wonderful. It's wonderful too that people don't have to work, like my parents did, God bless them.

Nurses who do such great work, don't have to ride bicycles, and I don't see dear Margery, struggling with a host of parcels, on hers. She knew what work was, as did so many I could recall. I thank God, the employees lot is much better. I am also grateful old people are given better pensions, they aren't adequate, but far better than sixty years ago. These dear souls, many of whom fought for our country, deserve to be looked after. It pleases me to, that the war dead of Veryan are still remembered, they made the supreme sacrifice, which we forget, at our peril. The hall, built by the boys who came back, from World War One still stands in their honour. Now the parish hall, and run by a committee, its well looked after.

Let's look now at the changes I don't like. Very old people, called by their first name, which shows a lack of respect, all too common now. Children being rude to teachers, who aren't allowed to correct them, the decline in standards, at every age, the decline of small shops, farms etc. Politics in local government, and politics in general. And above all, the demands for more and more money, which I consider is the biggest curse of society today. Money is fine, if used properly, during my early years, we had so little, now I see so much wasted.

What a difference!

With it all folk aren't so content, or happy, as in those days, maybe we have too much. I look back at the old days with much thought and feel I grew up, on balance, in good times. Sixty years ago, one could walk the roads with no fear of being knocked down by a car, and leave a door wide open while you went to the village, without being burgled.

Taking everything into consideration, I honestly feel, they were good days. One thing is certain, I wouldn't want to be a child now, for they have everything, but no freedom. In many respects, the old ways of doing things were best, with the world today gone completely mad, and the human race hasn't learnt the lessons of two world wars.

So as I've finished my sermon, its time for the last Hymn. In these troubled times, this one line seems to sum up my feelings:

Make Me A Channel Of Your Peace.

Mr Lenton, a fine old gentleman who is nearly 100, came to live in Veryan a few years ago

David Pearce, the author's great friend. One of a large family, he joined the Royal Marines and became a gentleman

David again, with his wife, Jean and the author

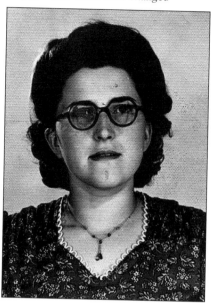

Beryl at 18. The elder of two evacuees who stayed with Frank's family in the early 40's

Miss Margery Johns carried the post for 30 years. Also pictured outside her door in Chapter 2

The shell of Ebenezer Chapel

*Hurricane lantern used
by farmers*

Frank Symons when at school

Triangle of grass today with trees gone (see page 62)

*Mr Walter Chenoweth, blacksmith
up until the Second World War*

Mrs Blamey and her son Jack

The school canteen built in the mid 1940's

*Frank's dad with Mrs Frost
a great Veryan character*

*Employees at the blacksmiths
before the War*

Rundles Walk, on land given in memory of a farmer who once owned it

Poultry running loose

An old fashioned lawnmower

A new estate built on farm land

Area opposite the school where the pupils used to have gardens

Tennis courts at the sports complex

A caravan – there are lots on the local campsite

Veryan School play area

A modern classroom at Veryan School

The Threshing Machine in action years ago

A more recent Threshing Machine

Mr Jack Blamey
Veryan through and through

Farmers put milk from their cows into churns, which were then collected by the Milk Marketing Board lorry

GREEN LANE, VERYAN.

Veryan Green − from the bottom end − prior to the bungalows being built

Triangle of grass outside Frank's shop before the trees were cut down circa 1910

Houses once known as Rundle's Row. Frank's shop now stands on the far left

Mr Bennett's class – Veryan School, 1947. Frank Symons extreme top left

Infants' class, Veryan School, 1940. Miss Walker in charge

Bowling at the sports centre

Melinsey Mill − the Hancock family run a business there